MUSICAL
INSTRUMENTS
OF THE WORLD

Flutes

Barrie Carson Turner

Illustrated by John See

🌣 Belitha Press

First published in the UK in 1998 by
Belitha Press Limited
London House, Great Eastern Wharf,
Parkgate Road, London SW11 4NQ

Text copyright © Barrie Carson Turner
Illustrations by John See
Copyright © in this format by Belitha Press Ltd

Editor: Claire Edwards
Series designer: Simeen Karim
Picture researcher: Juliet Duff
Educational consultant: Celia Pardaens

ISBN 1 85561 789 7

Printed in Hong Kong / China

British Library Cataloguing in Publication Data
for this book is available from the British Library.

9 8 7 6 5 4 3 2 1

Picture acknowledgements James Davis Travel Photography:
27; the Defence Picture Library: 8; Eye Ubiquitous: 23;
Robert Harding Picture Library: 14, 16; The Hutchison
Library: 15 Michael MacIntyre; The Japan Archive: 11;
Magnum Photos: 9, 12 Burt Glinn; Performing Arts Library:
13, 21, 28-29 Clive Barda; Redferns: 22 Brian Shuel; Peter
Sanders Photography: 26; Trip: 4-5 P. Rauter. 6-7 G. Horner;
Tropix: 25; John Walmsley Photo Library: 18, 19

Contents

Musical

Musical instruments are played in every country of the world. There are many thousands of different instruments of all shapes and sizes. They are often grouped into four families: strings, brass, percussion and woodwind.

Brass and woodwind instruments are blown to make their sound. Percussion instruments are struck (hit), shaken or scraped to make their sound. String instruments sound when their strings vibrate.

instruments

This book is about flutes, which are part of the woodwind family. Some flutes, like the piccolo and the suling, are played in orchestras. Others, such as the fife, are played in marching bands. You will often hear the sports whistle on the playing field.

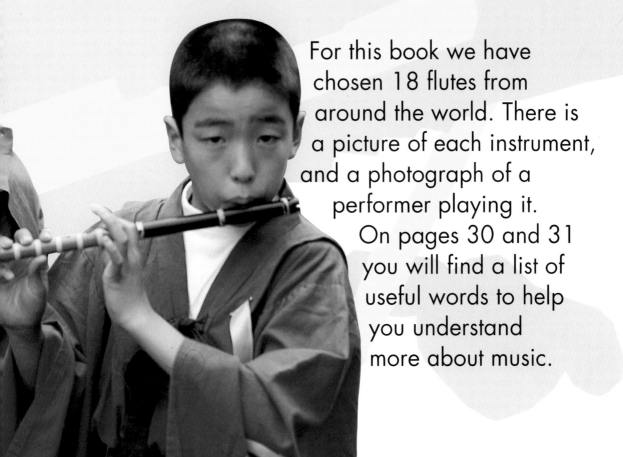

For this book we have chosen 18 flutes from around the world. There is a picture of each instrument, and a photograph of a performer playing it.

On pages 30 and 31 you will find a list of useful words to help you understand more about music.

Flute

The flute is an important instrument in an orchestra. Flutes were once made of wood, but today they are usually made of metal – sometimes even silver or gold. The mouthpiece is at one end of the instrument. Here the metal is shaped to make a resting place for the lips. The player blows across (not into) the blow hole. Each finger hole is covered by a small metal cap called a key.

key

foot joint

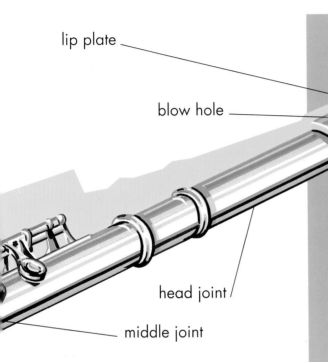

lip plate

blow hole

head joint

middle joint

The player makes different notes by pressing down the keys. The flute is built in three sections, called joints, so the instrument can be taken apart and carried easily. Flute players are called flautists.

The flute often plays the tune in a piece of music. Its low notes are rich and mellow. Its high notes are bright and powerful.

Bosun's pipe

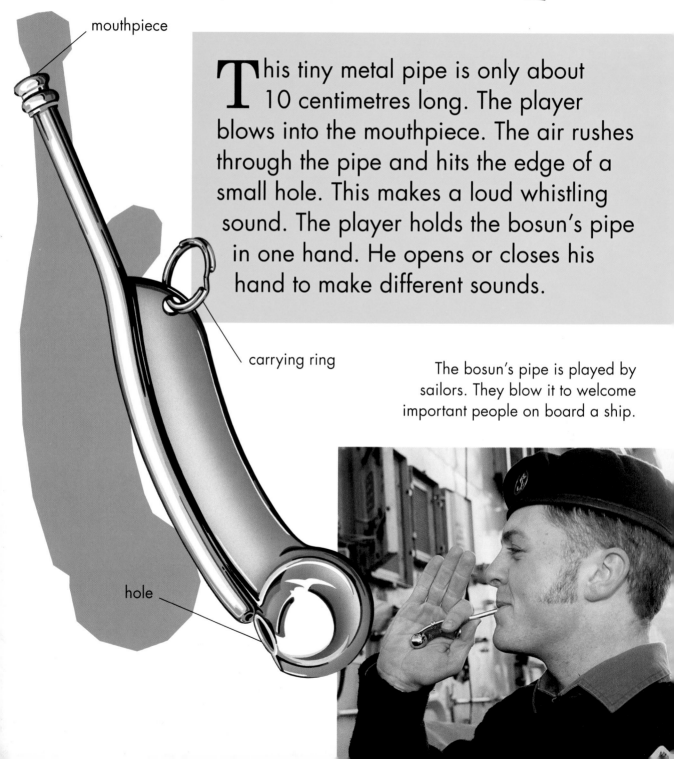

mouthpiece

This tiny metal pipe is only about 10 centimetres long. The player blows into the mouthpiece. The air rushes through the pipe and hits the edge of a small hole. This makes a loud whistling sound. The player holds the bosun's pipe in one hand. He opens or closes his hand to make different sounds.

carrying ring

The bosun's pipe is played by sailors. They blow it to welcome important people on board a ship.

hole

Di

The di (ti) has been played in China for more than a thousand years. It is made from bamboo, and is blown through a hole near one end. A thin piece of tissue paper is pasted over one of the holes. When the flute is blown, the paper adds a buzzing note to the flute sound.

blow hole

bamboo tube

tissue paper

finger hole

In ancient times, the di was often carved with a dragon's head at one end and a tail at the other end. Now it is usually made in a simple style.

Shakuhachi

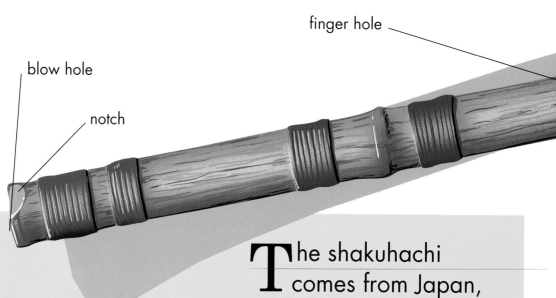

finger hole

blow hole

notch

The shakuhachi comes from Japan, and is traditionally played by men. It is made from bamboo, which is cut near the bottom of the plant where the stem becomes wider. This gives the instrument its curving shape. The player rests the instrument on his lower lip, and blows against a small notch cut into the side of the tube. The shakuhachi makes a beautiful clear sound.

At one time the shakuhachi was played by priests, who also used the instrument as a weapon of self-defence. It is still popular in Japan today and is played in classical and folk music.

In the past shakuhachi players had to wear baskets over their heads, so that no one recognized them. Today players still wear baskets over their heads when they play.

Fife

The fife is usually made of wood. It is held in the same way as the flute, out to the side of the player. It has a high shrill sound. The player makes different notes by covering the finger holes. On some fifes the finger holes are covered by metal caps called keys.

blow hole

lip plate

finger hole

Today the fife is often played in the USA, in marching bands. The bands play the same music that soldiers marched to hundreds of years ago.

Piccolo

The piccolo is a small flute. It is made of wood, metal, or both. It plays the highest notes in the orchestra, and makes a loud sound that can be heard above all the other instruments. Small metal caps called keys cover the finger holes. The player presses down the keys to make different notes.

blow hole

The piccolo is held and played like the flute. Piccolo is an Italian word that means small.

key

Nose flute

Nose flutes are mainly played in South-east Asia. The top end of the flute is held against the nose and blown through one nostril, while the thumb holds the other closed. In some countries, people believe that breath blown from the nose is magical, so the nose flute is often played at religious ceremonies.

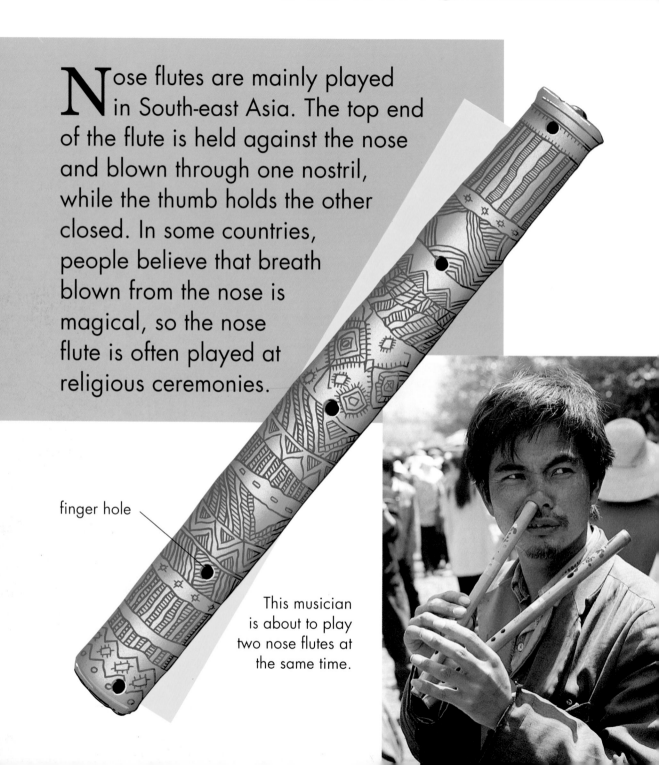

finger hole

This musician is about to play two nose flutes at the same time.

Suling

palm leaf ring

The suling is made from bamboo, and comes from Indonesia. It is sometimes called a ring flute because it has a ring of palm leaves wrapped round the blow hole. This helps to direct the player's breath into the hole. Some players can blow out at the same time as they breathe in. This is called circular breathing.

finger hole

Sulings are made in different sizes. They are usually played with a group of percussion instruments called a gamelan orchestra.

15

Recorder

Recorders have been played in Europe for hundreds of years. They have a soft tone, and must be blown very gently. They sound better played in small groups or as a solo instrument, rather than in an orchestra. There are five instruments in the recorder family. The highest is the sopranino. This is a tiny recorder with finger holes very close together.

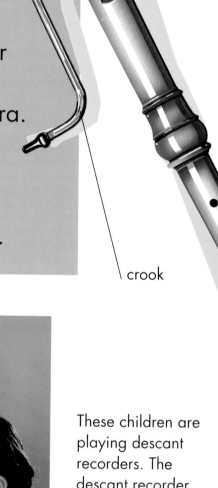

crook

These children are playing descant recorders. The descant recorder is the instrument most often played in schools.

family

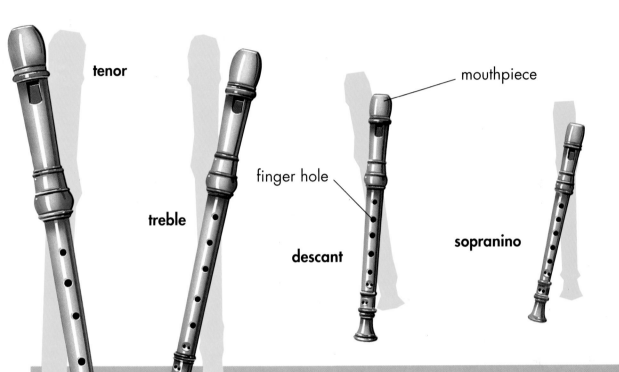

tenor

treble

mouthpiece

finger hole

descant

sopranino

The descant recorder is the next
highest instrument. The treble and tenor
are bigger and lower-sounding recorders.
The large bass recorder plays very low notes.
It is so big it has an extra metal tube called
a crook, so the player can reach the finger holes.

bass

Swannee whistle

mouthpiece

The swannee whistle has no finger holes. Instead, the different notes are made by a plunger held in the right hand. As the plunger is pushed in, the notes slide higher. As the plunger is pulled out the notes slide lower. No one knows how the swannee whistle got its name.

plunger

The notes on a swannee whistle slide up and down with a whooping sound. Because of this it is sometimes used in music for funny films.

18

Nightingale

M ost flutes are tube-shaped, but the nightingale is shaped like a bird. First it is filled with water. Then the player blows down a spout in the bird's tail. The air bubbles through the water and escapes through a small hole in the bird's head.

air escape hole

beak

blow spout

This nightingale is made of clay. It makes a low warbling sound, just like a bird. Plastic nightingales make a higher sounding whistle.

19

Panpipes

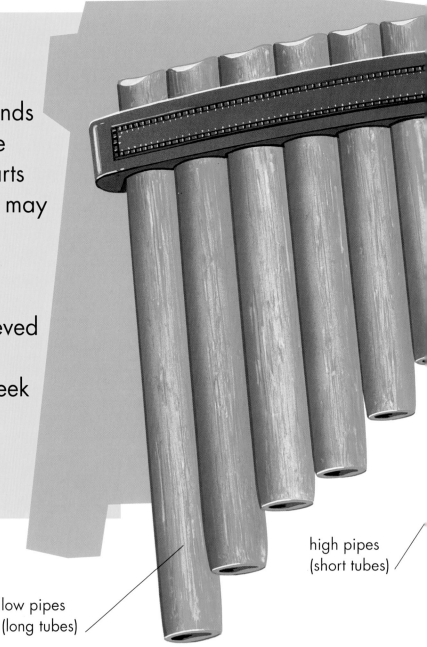

The panpipes have been played for thousands of years. They are found in many parts of the world, and may be made of reed, bamboo, wood, stone, or pottery. People once believed the pipes were invented by a Greek god called Pan, so they called the pipes panpipes.

high pipes
(short tubes)

low pipes
(long tubes)

Each pipe in a set of panpipes is a tiny flute that plays only one note. The pipes that make up the instrument are different lengths.

The long ones make low sounds and the short ones make high sounds. The pipes are usually tied together in a bundle or made into a raft shape.

This player is from South America, where the panpipes are very popular. Players blow across the tops of the pipes to make a light reedy sound.

21

Tin whistle

The tin whistle is very like the recorder, but is made of metal. It has only six finger holes and no thumb hole. In the past, the tin whistle was often played by street musicians. People would give the player a penny, which is why the tin whistle is also called a penny whistle.

The tin whistle has a bright, high-pitched sound. This makes it ideal for playing lively dance tunes, such as reels and jigs.

mouthpiece

finger hole

Sports whistle

The sports whistle is blown through a short, wide tube called a duct. At the other end of the tube the air hits the sharp edge of a long, narrow hole in the metal body. This makes a loud, shrill sound. There is a small clay pea inside the whistle, which adds a warble to the tone.

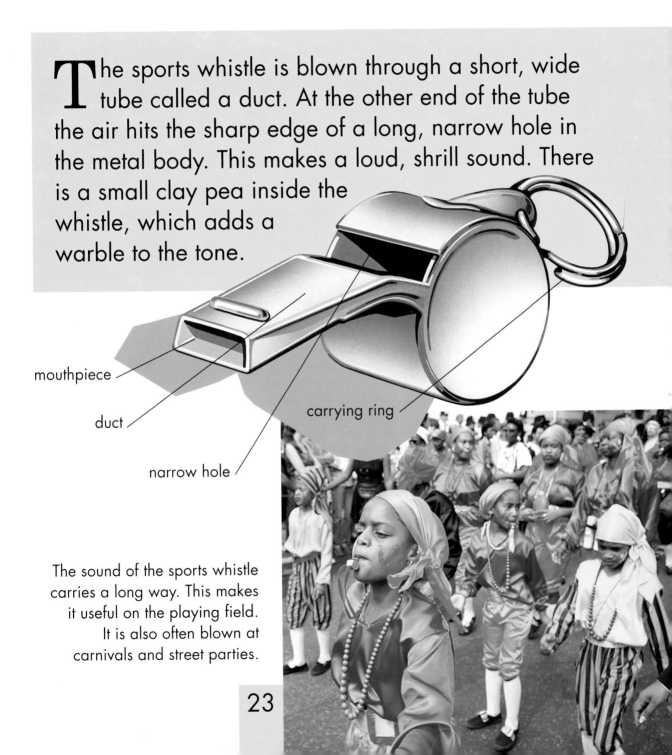

mouthpiece

duct

carrying ring

narrow hole

The sound of the sports whistle carries a long way. This makes it useful on the playing field. It is also often blown at carnivals and street parties.

23

Ocarina

Most flutes are shaped like a tube, but the ocarina is usually round or shaped like a long egg. Small ocarinas make high sounds, and large ones make low sounds. Some ocarinas have a tuning plunger. When this is pushed in or pulled out it makes the instrument sound higher or lower.

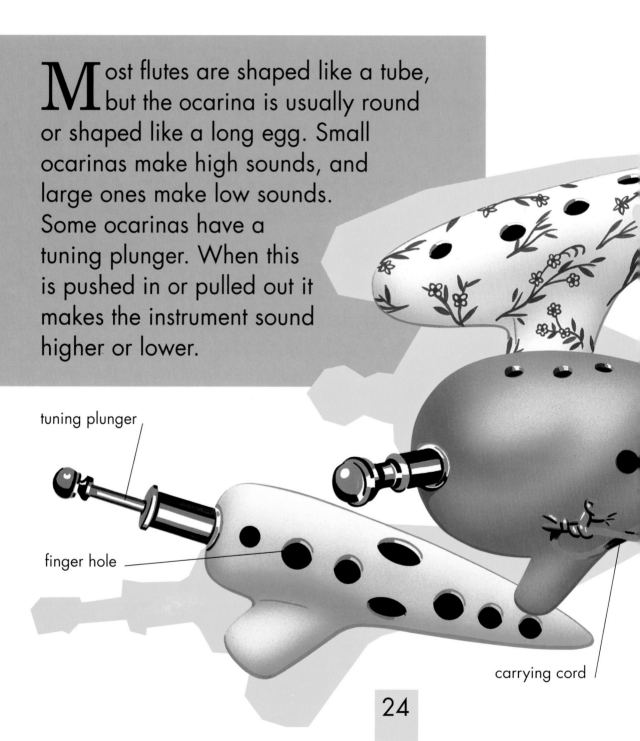

tuning plunger

finger hole

carrying cord

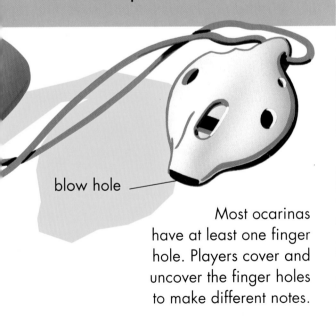

Ocarinas were first played thousands of years ago. At first they were made from bones, large hollow seeds and other natural objects. Now they can be made of clay, china, and even plastic. The word ocarina is Italian, and means little goose. They were called this because in Italy ocarinas were shaped like a bird.

blow hole —

Most ocarinas have at least one finger hole. Players cover and uncover the finger holes to make different notes.

25

Nay

The nay is a very old instrument, played thousands of years ago in Ancient Egypt. Today it is still played in Egypt and other nearby countries. The nay is made from bamboo, wood or metal, and the longest nays are a metre long. The player makes different notes by covering the finger holes and by moving his lips as he blows.

finger hole

The nay rests on the bottom lip. The player blows across the top edge of the instrument to make a soft reedy tone.

Double flute

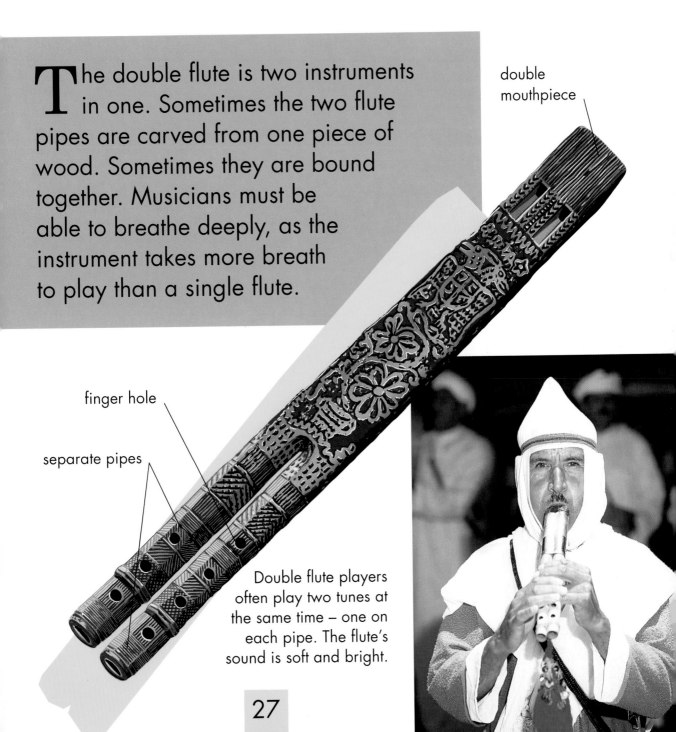

The double flute is two instruments in one. Sometimes the two flute pipes are carved from one piece of wood. Sometimes they are bound together. Musicians must be able to breathe deeply, as the instrument takes more breath to play than a single flute.

double mouthpiece

finger hole

separate pipes

Double flute players often play two tunes at the same time – one on each pipe. The flute's sound is soft and bright.

27

Bass flute

Bass (base) flutes are made of metal. They are very heavy, and so long that they have to be bent round at one end so the player can reach all the finger holes. Each finger hole is covered by a small metal cap called a key.

The bass flute plays very low notes. A bass flute player is called a bass flautist.

Players press down the keys to make different notes. The blow hole has a lip rest which allows players to rest their lips comfortably as they play. Players blow against the edge of the blow hole, not into it. The bass flute is played in an orchestra, but composers do not often write music for this instrument.

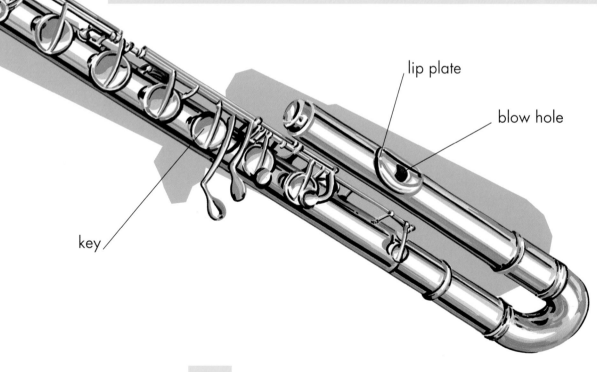

lip plate

blow hole

key

Words to

bamboo A kind of tall grass with a hard, hollow stem.

blow hole The hole into which a player blows to play a flute.

body The main part of an instrument.

carnival A festival held outdoors, like a party, with music and dancing in the street.

crook A piece of tubing on some long instruments, with the mouthpiece at the end. It allows players to reach all the finger holes as they blow.

duct The long front part of a flute mouthpiece.

family (of instruments) Instruments that are similar to each other.

finger holes The holes a player covers to make different notes on an instrument.

flute An instrument usually made in the shape of a tube. It is blown to make a sound.

folk music Popular songs or tunes so old, no one knows who wrote them.

gamelan orchestra An orchestra from Indonesia, made up of many different instruments.

joint A part of a flute or pipe. The joints fit together to make the whole instrument. A joint is also the point at which the parts join.

key A small metal cap covering a finger hole on a wind instrument.

lip rest A rest for the player's lips that makes it easier to blow down an instrument.

marching band A group of musicians who play military (soldiers') music as they march along.

remember

mellow A word used to describe a soft, warm, gentle sound.

musician Someone who plays an instrument or sings.

mouthpiece The part of a wind instrument held in the mouth, and where it is blown.

notch A V-shaped cut. A notch at the top of a flute makes it easier to blow.

orchestra A large group of musicians playing together.

performer Someone who plays or sings to other people.

pipe In music some flutes are also called pipes. A pipe is one of the tubes that makes up the panpipes.

plunger The part of a swannee whistle that is pushed in and pulled out to make different notes.

reedy A word used to describe a low, buzzing sound.

shrill A word used to describe a sound that is high and loud.

solo A piece of music played or sung by one player or singer.

street musician A performer who plays in the street for money. A street musician is also called a busker.

tone How an instrument sounds. For instance an instrument may have a bright tone, or a dull tone.

tuning plunger A tube that is pushed in or pulled out of an ocarina to change the notes it can play.

vibrate To move up and down very quickly, like shaking.

whistle A very high-sounding flute, or a very shrill sound.

Index